Timeline of the Roman Colosseum*

96
Colosseum completed.

399
Emperor Honorius bans gladiator training schools.

A.D. 72
Construction begins on Colosseum.

200
Women gladiators banned from the Colosseum.

422
Earthquake damages Colosseum; repaired A.D. 467 and 472.

80
First gladiatorial games at the Colosseum.

320
Colosseum is struck by lightning; remarkably, it is basically unharmed.

c. 404
Christian monk Telemachus leaps into the Colosseum arena to try to stop fights. He is executed.

c. 110
St. Ignatius of Antioch is the first-known Christian martyr to be killed in the Colosseum.

508
Further earthquake damage.

735
The Venerable Bede, a Christian monk, is first to record the name "Colosseum" in writing.

2000
Colosseum's seven-year restoration project completed.

c.590
Colosseum arena overgrown by grass.

1320
Colosseum clearly shown in first known medieval drawing of the city of Rome.

523
Last wild-animal show in Colosseum.

1084
Normans invade Rome and devastate area around the Colosseum.

1890s
Area around Colosseum cleared of other buildings.

604
Grass growing on Colosseum walls.

1400
Colosseum stone used for new buildings in Rome.

The Roman Empire

The map below shows the Roman Empire at its greatest size, under Emperor Trajan (A.D. 98–117). He added the province of Dacia (modern Romania) and land in the Middle East. At its height, the Roman Empire covered the land of about 30 of today's countries and had some 50 million people living within its borders. Trajan's successor, Hadrian, thought the empire was growing too big to defend. He stopped the expansion and tried to consolidate and fortify Roman lands.

Rome, the capital of the empire, was the biggest, grandest, and busiest city in the Roman world. It had grown from tiny settlements dating from around 800 B.C. In A.D. 64, during Nero's reign, the city was devastated by fire. It was rebuilt and enlarged, but it was not until A.D. 271 that strong defensive walls were built. These were called the Aurelian Walls.

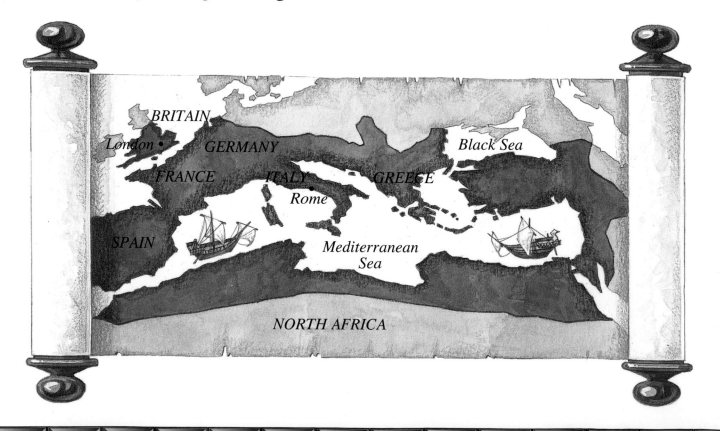

Author:

John Malam studied ancient history and archaeology at the University of Birmingham, after which he worked as an archaeologist at the Ironbridge Gorge Museum, Shropshire. He is now an author, specializing in information books for children. He lives in Cheshire with his wife, a book designer, and their two children.

Artist:

Dave Antram was born in Brighton, England, in 1958. He studied at Eastbourne College of Art and then worked in advertising for 15 years before becoming a full-time artist. He has illustrated many children's non-fiction books.

Series Creator:

David Salariya was born in Dundee, Scotland. He has illustrated a wide range of books and has created and designed many new series for publishers both in the U.K. and overseas. In 1989 he established The Salariya Book Company. He lives in Brighton with his wife, the illustrator Shirley Willis, and their son.

Editor:

Karen Barker Smith

© The Salariya Book Company Ltd MMXIII

No part of this publication may be reproduced in whole or in part, or stored in a retrieval system, or transmitted in any form or by any means, electronic, mechanical, photocopying, recording, or otherwise, without written permission of the publisher. For information regarding permission, write to the copyright holder.

Published in Great Britain in 2013 by
The Salariya Book Company Ltd
25 Marlborough Place, Brighton BN1 1UB

ISBN-13: 978-0-531-27503-0 (lib. bdg.)   978-0-531-28028-7 (pbk.)

All rights reserved.
Published in 2013 in the United States
by Franklin Watts
An imprint of Scholastic Inc.
Published simultaneously in Canada.

A CIP catalog record for this book is available
from the Library of Congress.

Printed and bound in Shanghai, China.
Printed on paper from sustainable sources.
Reprinted in   MMXVII.
9   10   R21   20   19   18   17

SCHOLASTIC, FRANKLIN WATTS, and associated logos are trademarks and/or registered trademarks of Scholastic Inc., 557 Broadway, New York, NY 10012.

You Wouldn't Want to Be a Roman Gladiator!

Gory Things You'd Rather Not Know

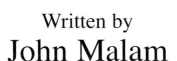

Written by
John Malam

Illustrated by
David Antram

Created and designed by
David Salariya

Franklin Watts®
An Imprint of Scholastic Inc.
NEW YORK • TORONTO • LONDON • AUCKLAND • SYDNEY
MEXICO CITY • NEW DELHI • HONG KONG
DANBURY, CONNECTICUT

Contents

Introduction

It is the 1st century A.D. and you live in a village in the Roman province of Gallia, which covers a large area of northern Europe. You don't like the Romans much, and they don't like you or your people. The fact is the Romans invaded your territory more than 100 years ago, as they have done in many places, to build up the huge Roman Empire. They plan on ruling over you for a long time to come and say your people are uncivilized. They call you "barbarians," meaning that you are different from them. The Romans believe they are much better than you.

From time to time some of your people pick a fight with the Romans. But you're no match against the Roman army. If you're not killed in battle, don't expect to be shown any mercy; you'll be taken prisoner and marched off to the

city of Rome. If you survive the long journey, you face an uncertain future. Will you be sold as a slave to a rich Roman citizen, or will you be sent to work in the mines? Will you end up doing hard labor in the quarries or will you sail around the Roman Empire as a galley slave?

Your fate is out of your control, but you can be sure of one thing — you wouldn't want to be a Roman gladiator!

Gotcha! Romans Get Their Man

Goodbye to Your Former Life:

WEAPONS. The Romans will destroy your weapons — your bronze shield, iron sword and dagger, and slingshot.

JEWELRY. The Romans will take your gold neckring, or torque, and bronze bracelets.

HORSE AND CHARIOT. The Romans will take your horses and smash your chariot.

HOME AND FAMILY. You may never see them again.

THE ROMAN ARMY has invaded Gallia. The Romans want to make it part of their growing empire, but first they must defeat troublemakers. The Gauls, the people of Gallia, live in many different tribes. Some tribes are happy for the Romans to be their rulers, but others fight them.

I hate Romans!

The Roman soldiers wear armor and follow a carefully worked-out battle plan. The Gauls fight bare-chested and are not as well organized. The fighting is soon over, and unfortunately for you, your tribe loses the battle. Captured Gauls have their weapons taken away, and the fittest become prisoners of war. You are one of the prisoners, and you are about to begin a new life.

Handy Hint

Before the battle, offer a gift to your gods by throwing a weapon into a bog. This is the entrance to their underground world.

What Next?

Prisoners are chained at the neck and led away to begin a new life as slaves.

Prisoners are marched hundreds of miles from Gallia to Rome, the heart of the Roman Empire.

I hate Gauls!

GALLIA

ROME

Sold! A Slave Market in Rome

It's a Hard Life for a Slave:

DOWN IN THE MINES. Some slaves are sent to work in mines. They may never see daylight again.

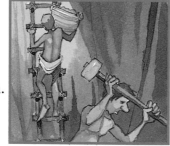

QUARRYING. Slaves also work in the heat and dust of quarries, breaking rock for buildings and sculptures.

GALLEY SLAVES. Some men will become galley slaves, rowing the Roman navy's fighting ships and being whipped if they stop.

FARMING. Slaves on farms work in all kinds of weather to grow food for the Romans.

AFTER CAPTURE by the army you are passed on to a slave dealer, who buys and sells slaves. The dealer takes you to a slave market, where you stand on a platform for everyone to see. Slaves with diseases are made to hold a sign so that people know there is something wrong with them. Chalk dust is sprinkled on your feet as a sign that you are a slave. The slave dealer asks people to call out prices, and he will sell you to the person who pays the most.

Before   After

A NEW MAN. Your new owner plans to turn you from a *Gallia comata*, Latin meaning a "hairy Gaul," into a civilized Roman gladiator.

Oh, No! Gladiators Go to School

Are You Ready for This?

NEW ARRIVAL. Your owner will hand you over to a trainer — a tough man who will teach you how to be a gladiator.

YOU ARE NOW the property of a wealthy Roman citizen. He's decided you will be sent to a *ludus gladiatorius* — a school where slaves, criminals, and other wretches are trained to fight as gladiators. Once inside, the gates will be locked and there will be no escape. You'll be trained to fight by a *lanista,* or "butcher," an old gladiator whose fighting days are over.

Before

After

GET FIT. You'll exercise every day with weights to build up your body's strength.

FAKE SWORD. Until you can be trusted with a real weapon, you will practice with a wooden sword.

Go for it! It won't fight back you know!

HOW TO FIGHT. You'll learn how to fight with a sword, practicing on a "man of straw." If you don't train hard enough, you'll feel the sting of a whip on your back.

Man of straw

Rr..i..p

Handy Hint

If you get injured, you must visit the school's excellent doctor. He'll dress your wounds, and then you'll be ready to continue training.

Who's Who:

THE STAFF

Trainer

Owner

Guard

Mortician

Accountant Armorer Cook Doctor

THE PUPILS

Get to know your place at the school. The staff members are the bossy Romans looking after you; the pupils are the dregs of society.

Slave Criminal Condemned man Bankrupt Roman

11

Locked In! Your New Family

Do You Have the Stomach For It?

Porridge

Barley grains

Beans

PORRIDGE. Every day the school cook will feed you barley, porridge, and boiled beans. Don't complain about boring, bland food — you'll get nothing else.

ASH. A few mouthfuls of dry, dusty ash are said to be good for building up the body. Just close your eyes and swallow. Don't choke!

TRAINING doesn't end when you hang up your sword at the end of the day. You'll go back to your barracks — a long, low wooden building. This is where you'll eat and sleep...and be locked in at night. Your trainer will come too and watch over you as you eat specially prepared gladiator food. The trainer thinks of the men in the barracks as his family, so he will make sure you are taken care of.

This stuff is only fit for dogs.

YOUR TRAINER. He takes great pride in seeing how weak-bodied slaves can be turned into muscle-bound fighting men — but only if they follow a strict, nourishing diet. It's no wonder that gladiators are sometimes called *hordearii*, which means "barley men."

Eat your porridge – you've got ash for dessert!

This isn't even fit for dogs!

Handy Hint

Troubled by aches and pains? Then visit the school *unctore*, who will massage your body.

MUSCLE MAN. Believe it or not, the school food really is good for you. All that porridge will give you muscles and strength.

13

Behave...or Be Punished

Punishments:

BRANDING. A runaway will have FHE (for *Fugitivus Hic Est*) and the initials of his owner, such as LT (for *Lucius Titius*), burned into his forehead. It means: "This man is the runaway slave of Lucius Titius."

FLOGGING. One hundred lashes of the whip will tear the skin from a runaway's back.

STOCKS. For a first offense you might be locked in the stocks for a week — time for you to learn to behave.

IT'S NO USE trying to escape, since the gladiators' school is surrounded by high walls and fences. You won't be able to climb over them without being spotted by the security guards. But if you attack a staff member, you will be punished. The school has a prison — a dark, rat-infested hole where prisoners are

I never thought I'd miss that porridge.

shackled and chained to the walls. If you're unlucky enough to be locked inside, eat whatever the guards give you — it might be days before you get your next rotten meal. If you cause trouble too often, your owner might sell you and you could end your days working in the mines. The choice is yours!

The prison has a low ceiling. There's not enough room to stand, so you have to lie or crouch on the ground.

On Parade! The Big Day Arrives

The Night Before:

BANQUET.
You will be given a splendid feast — as much good food as you can eat. There will be meat and wine — definitely no porridge.

PUBLIC. The public views the gladiators at their banquet. They look for men they think will fight well in the games — not for those who won't.

SAY GOODBYE. At the banquet, some gladiators plead with the public to take final messages to their families.

WHEN YOUR TRAINING is over, it is time for you to face the toughest challenge of your life. Your owner will take you, together with his other gladiators, to perform in the games. You will arrive in town the day before the games begin to have time to recover from the journey. That night you will be treated to a splendid meal. Enjoy it — it might be your last. On the day of the games you will march into the arena and parade before the emperor. Remember, you are a gladiator — a courageous fighting man. Do not show any fear. There is silence as you call out the traditional words spoken by gladiators before the contest begins (right).

ADVERTISEMENTS. Notices painted on walls announce the games. Street criers call out the names of the gladiators.

BANNERS. Men carry painted banners with details about the games to let everyone know they are about to begin.

Who's Who in the Arena?

What You Will Need:

Weapons

Spear

Trident

Net

Lasso

Dagger

Sword

Armor

Helmet

Greaves

Chain mail

Shields

Gladiators

ANDABATUS.
Wears a helmet with no eye holes. Charges blindly on horseback at an opponent.

ESSEDARIUS.
A gladiator who drives a horse-drawn chariot.

RETARIUS.
Tries to snare an opponent in his net. Left arm and shoulder are protected by armor.

MYRMILLO.
Carries a dagger and shield. Wears a wide leather belt and leg bands.

THRACIAN.
Uses a small shield and a curved dagger. Wears greaves on both legs.

IN YOUR TRAINING you will have learned how to fight as one particular type of gladiator. Perhaps you were trained to fight as a lightly armored *retarius*, or "net man." Or maybe your skills as an *essedarius* — a chariot fighter — will be called upon. It has cost your owner a lot of money to buy you, feed, train, and equip you for the contest. Now you must be victorious — winning is all that matters. If you lose, you die. So, be brave! Fight, conquer…and live!

Handy Hint

Make sure you have an attendant to see to your needs. Let him carry your equipment into the arena.

SAMNITE. Wears a visored helmet with crest. Carries a sword and a large shield.

DIMACHAERIUS. Fights with two swords and wears little armor.

LAQUERIUS. Similar to a *retarius* but with a lasso instead of a net.

SECUTOR. A lightly armed fighter who chases his opponent.

VELITUS. Armed with only a spear.

WOMAN. An uncommon sight, but women fight as gladiators too.

Fight! Gladiators in Action

Secutor gladiator

THE GAMES are about to begin. Your moment of glory is upon you — you hope. But first, you must entertain the crowd by fighting with blunt, wooden swords. Music sounds, and your practice sword is taken from you and replaced with a real weapon. You are about to fight for your life, but it is not just your opponent you have to worry about.

Your trainer will be watching every move, and if he thinks you are not trying hard enough, he has a painful way of prodding you back into action.

This will teach you to run from a fight!

Prepare to Fight

As you prepare for your fight, the arena will be buzzing with excitement. Don't let your nerves get the better of you — the show must go on!

WARM-UP FIGHT. First you'll fight with wooden swords in a practice duel.

GAMBLING. Spectators will gamble on whether you will win your fight …or not.

OPPONENT. You will be drawn to fight against another gladiator.

20

Retarius gladiator

Handy Hint

Keep on fighting — if you don't, your trainer will send a slave to whip you or prod you with a hot poker.

Fight, you lazy dog!

REAL WEAPON. You will be given your real weapon — no more wooden swords from now on.

MUSIC. Musicians will play war trumpets, pipes, and flutes.

ACTION! The contest begins — it's a fight to the death.

NOISY CROWD. The crowd will cheer and shout all the time you are fighting.

Ouch! Let Him Have It!

BAD LUCK! In your contest you were drawn to fight a *retarius*, a gladiator who catches opponents in his net before moving in for the kill. As you lie on the sandy floor of the arena, he brings his dagger to your throat. You must think fast — you may have only seconds to live. The crowd is on its feet, shouting "*Habet, hoc habet!*" which means "Got him! Let him have it!" There's only one thing you can do: Appeal to the emperor. As you raise your left hand, the emperor will turn to the crowd and let it decide your fate. All you can hope for is that it calls out "*Mitte!*" — "Let him go!"

Will You Live or Die?

EMPEROR APPEAL. A fallen gladiator can appeal to the emperor by raising one finger on his left hand. The emperor will ask the crowd what it wants.

THUMBS UP. If the people hold their thumbs up and wave their handkerchiefs, the fallen gladiator will be allowed to live.

THUMBS DOWN. If the people turn their thumbs to the ground, as if swiping a sword through the air, then the defeated man must die.

A DRAW. If both gladiators are still on their feet and have fought their best, then a draw may be declared and neither man will die.

Splash! A Sea Battle

Who Are You?

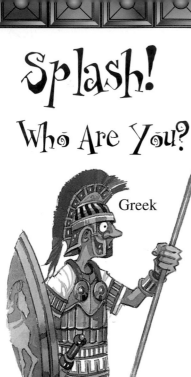

Greek

Persian

ENEMIES. The Greek and Persian peoples were sworn enemies.

I'S AN AMAZING SIGHT to see the arena flooded to make a lake. Water is piped in from a pool outside, then battleships called triremes float gracefully across it. A sea battle is about to begin,

Fighting at Sea:

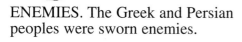

LONG AND SHORT RANGE. From a distance, you will shoot burning arrows at the enemy ship. Then, when you are upon them, you will use hand weapons.

BATTERING RAM. The prow of a trireme is fitted with a bronze battering ram to smash into and sink other ships.

based on one fought between the Greeks and the Persians about 300 years ago. To entertain the crowd, you will dress as either a Greek or Persian soldier. A sea battle is a great spectacle, so play your part well.

Handy Hint

Learn to swim. Even though the water is shallow, you could still drown.

Prepare to perish, Persians!

Growl! Attacked by Beasts

You Will Need:

BESTIARIUS. A gladiator trained to hunt wild beasts.

AFTER THE SEA BATTLE, the water is drained from the arena and another scene is set. The arena will become a park, with trees, rocky outcrops, and wild beasts brought from Africa and other Roman provinces. An animal hunt will take place, where hunters stalk their prey with dogs and weapons. You must take great care — the animals are savage, hungry beasts.

Some *bestiarii* use weapons, but those who are criminals have no means of defense.

Aaargh!

WEAPONS. You hunt with spears, arrows, daggers, nets, and fierce hunting dogs.

Beware of the Animals:

The arena will contain lions and tigers, which can be taught to lick their tamer's hands, and elephants that kneel before the emperor.

Handy Hint

Know your escape routes! Look for a pole to climb up, a wall to jump over, or a cage to take shelter inside.

Grrrr

Down, boy...

Grrr...Grrrr

Let me at him! Let me at him!

27

It's Over! The Games End

T SEEMS THE CROWD showed you no mercy, and the *retarius* was the winner of the contest. While your body is dragged from the arena, the victorious gladiator is presented with his prizes. At the end of the games, officials write up the record books, putting letters next to the names of the competitors: "P" means the person perished, "V" stands for victor, and "M" indicates that the gladiator lived to fight another day.

If You Are Still Alive...

PRIZES. Palm branches, silver dishes, and gold are given to the gladiators who survive the games.

BACK FOR MORE. The owner of a winning gladiator will enter him in further contests.

At the End of the Day

CLEANERS. Slaves rake the sand over to remove all signs of blood.

Victor today – back to porridge tomorrow!

DRAGGED AWAY. Men drag away the bodies of the dead and dump them in a pit.

FINISHED OFF. Dying gladiators are killed by a man dressed as the mythical character Charon from the Underworld.

Handy Hint

After many victories, a gladiator might be presented with a wooden sword. His fighting days will end, and he can become a trainer at a gladiator school.

Glossary

Arena The building where gladiatorial games were held. It literally means "sand" — a reference to the sand-covered floor.

Barbarian Anyone who was not a Roman. An uncivilized person.

Barracks The building in which gladiators lived while at training school.

Bestiarius A beast fighter trained to hunt wild animals in the arena.

Chain mail A type of armor made from small interlocking rings of metal.

Charon The ferryman who the Romans believed took the souls of the dead from the land of the living to the Underworld.

Galley A type of ship rowed by slaves.

Gallia An area of northern Europe where the present-day countries of France and Belgium are.

Games A form of public entertainment involving gladiators.

Gaul A member of one of the tribes that lived in Gallia.

Gladiator A man (or, very occasionally, a woman) trained to fight for the entertainment of others.

Greave A leg protector, usually made of metal, worn over the lower leg.

Hordearii A popular name for gladiators meaning "barley men," due to the barley porridge they were fed.

Lanista A man who trained or taught others to become gladiators.

Lasso A length of rope with a loop, used to catch an opponent.

Ludus gladiatorius A school or camp where gladiators lived and were trained to fight.

Man of straw A post, sack, or framework that a gladiator practiced using his weapons against.

Mortician An undertaker. A person whose job is to organize funerals.

Prow The front of a ship.

Sestertii Coins used in Roman currency.

Slave collar A name tag worn by a slave that stated whom he or she belonged to.

Slingshot A hand-held weapon that hurled a small stone over a long distance.

Torque A loop of metal, often bronze or gold, worn around the neck as an item of jewelry.

Trident A three-pronged fishing spear.

Trireme A battleship of the Roman, Greek, and Persian navies.

Unctore A person whose job it was to massage, or rub, soothing oils into someone's body.

Underworld The world of the dead according to Roman belief.

Index

A
andabatus (gladiator) 18
animal hunt 26
appeal 22
arena 16, 18, 19, 20, 22, 24, 26, 28, 30
armorer 11
ash 12

B
banquet 16
barbarians 5, 30
barracks 12, 30
battering ram 24
battleships 24
bestiarius (beast fighter) 26, 30
branding 14

C
chain mail 18, 30
chariot 6, 18
Charon 28, 30
cook 11, 12
criminals 10-11, 23

D
dimachaerius (gladiator) 19
doctor 11
dogs 26

E
emperor 16-17, 22, 27
essedarius (gladiator) 18

F
family 6, 12, 16
farming 8
flogging 14
food 12-13, 16

G
galley 5, 8, 30
Gallia 5, 6-7, 30
gambling 20

games 16, 20, 28, 30
Gauls 6-7, 30
gladiators, types of 18-19
gods 7
greaves 18, 30
Greeks 25
guards 11, 14-15

H
helmet 18
hordearii (barley men) 13, 30

J
jewelry 6, 31

L
lanista (trainer) 10, 31
laquerius (gladiator) 19
lasso 18, 19, 31
ludus gladiatorius (gladiator school) 10, 31

M
man of straw 11, 31
mines 5, 8, 15
mortician 11, 31
myrmillo (gladiator) 18

N
navy 8
net man 19

O
owner 10-11, 15, 16, 19, 28

P
parade 16
Persians 25
porridge 12-13, 16
prison 14-15
prisoners 5, 7, 14
prizes 28
punishments 9, 14-15

R
retarius (gladiator) 18-19, 21, 22, 28
Roman citizen 10
Roman Empire 6-7
Rome 5, 7
runaways 14

S
samnite (gladiator) 19
school 11, 12, 14, 29
sea battle 24-25
secutor (gladiator) 19, 20
slave collar 9, 31
slave market 8-9
slaves 7, 8, 10-11, 13, 21
spectators 20
stocks 14
sword 11, 12, 18

T
thracian (gladiator) 18
thumbs down 22
thumbs up 22
torque 6, 31
trainer 10-11, 12-13, 20, 29
training 10-11, 16
trident 18, 31
trireme 24, 31

U
unctore 13, 31
Underworld 29, 30, 31

V
velitus (gladiator) 19

W
weapons 6-7, 10, 18, 22, 24
whip 11, 14, 21
women 19
wooden sword 10, 20-21, 29

Ancient Roman Life

The Roman Empire
In 27 B.C., after many years of civil war, Caesar's adopted son, Augustus, seized power. He became emperor, the ruler in charge of Rome and the lands it controlled. Augustus was a wise and just leader. When he died in A.D. 14, he was declared a god and a temple was erected in his honor.

Travel and Trade
Rome was the center of a huge empire. The rest of Italy counted as a province of the empire, even though Rome stood in its midst. The excellent road system and the peace and safety of the times, known as the *Pax Romana* (Roman peace), encouraged more people to travel and trade abroad. Archeological evidence shows the Romans traded throughout the Mediterranean. They took Roman customs and culture with them, and also adopted new practices, such as Christianity, from the east.

The Army
The Roman army was a huge, well-trained, well-disciplined, highly successful military machine. There could not have been a Roman Empire without it. The army also offered young recruits a good career, with decent pay and conditions and a chance to see more of the empire. The only catch was that a person had to sign up for 25 years. Roman citizens joined as legionaries (professional soldiers); noncitizens as auxiliaries (supporting troops). Young noblemen often joined up as the first step in a political career.

City and Country
Many Romans lived in large, crowded cities throughout the empire. The majority, however, lived and worked in the countryside, mostly as poor farmers. Others worked on the estates of rich landowners who lived in the cities and visited their estates occasionally. The main crops were the staple ingredients of the Roman diet: olives for oil, grapes for wine, and grain for bread.

The population of Rome was growing so fast that grain had to be imported, much of it from Egypt.

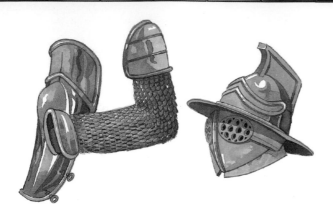

Slaves

Without slaves, the Roman Empire would have ground to a halt. Slaves did all the hardest and dirtiest work, as well as waiting on the wealthy. Most were prisoners of war. Greek slaves were often well educated, so they were highly prized as teachers and doctors. Some slaves were treated well and eventually given their freedom. Others became very influential as secretaries to senators or even emperors. Most of them, however, led miserable lives.

Language

Many different languages were spoken throughout the Roman Empire, but the official language was Latin. This helped bring some unity to the various parts of the empire. Educated Romans also learned Greek.

Latin is still studied today, and it is still the offical language of the Roman Catholic Church. Here are a few words to learn: *Salve!* (Hello!) and *Vale!* (Good-bye!). *O me miserum!* (Woe is me!) is a useful phrase if you're feeling down.

Did You Know?

• The amount of meat or fish that people ate depended on what they could afford. Pork and mutton were popular meats, though more exotic dishes, such as flamingo, were served at banquets.

• Cabbage was one of the most popular plant remedies. It was crushed and spread on bruises and boils; stewed for headaches; fried in hot fat to treat sleeplessness; dried, powdered, and sniffed to clear stuffed noses; and squeezed to extract juice to use as eardrops!

Roman Emperors

Julius Caesar In 47 B.C., a successful general named Julius Caesar declared himself dictator. Many people feared that he was trying to end the republic and rule like the old kings. Caesar was murdered in 44 B.C. by a group of his political enemies, including his old friend Marcus Brutus. After his death, there were many years of civil war.

Caligula's Rule Caligula squandered the riches of Rome. He believed he was a god and dressed up as Apollo, Venus, Mercury, and Hercules. He exiled his own wife and outraged senators when he insisted on having his horse elected consul and priest—one of the highest political positions! Once, at the Circus Maximus, the gladiatorial games ran out of criminals, and the next event was the lions, Caligula's favorite. He ordered his guards to drag the first five rows of spectators into the arena, which they did. These hundreds of people were all devoured for his own amusement.

The Madness of Nero The Emperor Nero was insane and cruel. Legend has it that he laughed and played music while watching a terrible fire that destroyed a large part of Rome. He also tried to kill his own mother by having her ship sunk, but when that failed he simply ordered her to be executed.

Commodus This emperor so adored the gladiatorial games that he personally entered some of them, fighting alongside the gladiators who were criminals and slaves. This deeply offended the entire empire, particularly the Senate. Commodus especially adored killing animals, and once killed 100 lions in one day, much to the spectators' disgust.